Reaching Out

Reaching Out

ROBERT MONDA

Locke Monda Publications

New York

For information about this title, to order more books
and/or electronic media, contact the publisher:

Locke Monda Publications
lockemondapublications@gmail.com
lockemondapublications.com

Library of Congress Control Number: 2021901396

ISBN: 978-0-578-84237-0

Printed in the United States of America

Cover and interior design: Robin Locke Monda

Locke Monda Publications
Staten Island, NY 10301

www.lockemondapublications.com

To my wife, Robin

CONTENTS

FERRIS WHEEL 3

I
AGAIN 7
BLACKOUT 9
DAYBREAK 10
DEPRESSION 11
ON A THEORY OF CAUSALITY 12
DOPPELGANGER 14
LAMENT 16
MY PRESENT CONDITION 17
AT TWENTY-FIVE 18

II
COMMON KNOWLEDGE 23
THE ICE AGE 25
FALL 26
LABOR DAY 27
COATS 29
THE MUSIC OF THE SPHERES 31
THE LION'S MOUTH 32
THE GATEKEEPER 34
DISILLUSION AT 2AM 36

III
THE CHICKEN COOPS OF LEWIS STREET 41
LAST YEAR'S OVERCOAT 44
THE COGNOSCENTI LAMENT THE DOLLAR'S DECLINE 46
TO SOMEONE I CANNOT SEE ANYMORE 48
TROUBLED SLEEP 50
STORM WARNING 51
MONDAY 52
NO BALLOONS 54
THE BURNING BED 55
PUSHING SIXTY 56

IV
DREAM OF MY FATHER 59
A FEW PHOTOGRAPHS 60
OLD MEN IN THE PARK 62
SALUTATIONS 63
WIRE MOMMY 64

V

TRAVELING THROUGH WYOMING   67
IN THE HEARTLAND   69
CAPE CHARLES LIBRARY   71
HEARING MISSISSIPPI FRED MCDOWELL   72
FREEDOM, NEW HAMPSHIRE   73
THE YEAR OF THE COMET   74

VI

SUB ROSA   77
THE CAT'S DIET   78
A SPARE RIB   79
MR. YEATS' SONG   80
THE SAILOR'S SONG   81
GENESIS   83
THE NET   84
WHILE YOU WAIT   85
REACHING OUT   86

VII

WHISKEY PRIEST   89
NEW STONE EGG   90
THE CLAY FOOT   92
COURTING THE MUSE, TWO VISITS   93
FRANKLIN'S KITE   96
CHINESE NOVEL   97
MEMBER OF THE FAMILY   98

THANK YOU   101

ABOUT THE TYPE   103

Ferris Wheel

They cut my block in half
to make a road
all the way to California,
and the Ferris wheel
doesn't come around anymore.
A team of horses pulled it
to the junk yard
where it sunk unwheeled,
a crumpled metal napkin
among the other wrecks.

Route 80 swims with cars.
The connecting multi-lane, intricate,
takes them past faster than the limit,
sixty cars a minute, day and night.
Listening to its rhythm,
the noise becomes a habit,
as with our south-end street,
complete with a tavern
and Ferris wheel
once a week on Saturdays.

It's convenient to have the highway
so near the house;
the mounting death toll
in the backyard

makes newspapers unnecessary,
and parents don't hear children
squabble for nickels,
or old folks complain about the music
as poor kids on the sidewalk watch
the wheel go round and round.

I

Again

The kids have made a fire in the back lot
with oily rags, cardboard boxes, an old end-table.
All day a sneaky plume of smoke rises
behind the house and drifts sideways
like a feather boa across the back alleys
where junk is stored in barrels and sheds,
and newspapers are bundled waiting to ignite.
The children are careless, see them leave
with their toys of monsters and spacemen.
In their imagination, they are on Mongo already
in a surface-craft that rockets to the conflagration.
Each child is a superhero with an insignia,
a noble lineage, a striking physique...
The back lot cannot be seen from here;
the damage done can only be guessed.
An acrid cloud chokes the neighbors,
maybe some rubble has caught flame.
By now the children are at some other game;
they do not hear the fire trucks pack the street,
the fire hoses screwed into the dry hydrants
and the faint glow that can be seen blocks away.
All day the firemen battle the blaze;
but the entire neighborhood is a shell,
the front of a movie set, a Potemkin village.
The children come back from their play
and are taken to a shelter; they will be forgiven,

they are young; it was our fault not to supervise,
to have pails of water to douse the flames.
The children have been washed and fed;
they have been dressed in a change of clothes,
and they're playing behind the shelter
with cardboard and matches, lumber and old tires,
but we don't have to worry,
for all this—this all—cannot possibly happen again.

Blackout

Sirens wail down the highway;
the radio sputters and dies,
lights go out
and the plant closes.
Hugging the road's shoulder,
I return home.

There is disorder here:
shadows prowl.
Stooped women
pull children from the porch
and disappear
behind locked doors.

I'm without power
like the Northeast Grid
snapped by an overload,
and blank
before an open telephone,
I fail to call.

A limb crashes in the yard;
among its branches, a wild duck
twitches a broken wing.
It won't survive until dawn.
The lights brown on
and cranes lift rubble from the roads.

Daybreak

An alarm rings insistently
on daylight savings time.
The fogged mirror
above the steaming sink
shows a face nearly worn off.
The lid on the honey jar has rusted
and the fork slips, notching a finger.
All is lost: the toast burns,
the smoke detector trips,
and blood spattered on the counter
forms in blots of a Rorschach test.
Call in sick, get into bed;
maybe, with lunch,
the omens will be more propitious.

Depression

When the child you thought was lost is crying, wailing inconsolably against a pile of damp leaves, huddled in the hole of a rotting tree, burrs on his clothing, stomach shooting with pain, just where you left him and walked away, walked away and thought you would never return, and again he has found you, a long lost dog, wet to the bone and bedraggled; when you open the door, having traveled a thousand miles; and you look for an old rug, some dry spot, where you can rub down this dog, or boy; and as you chop the celery and carrots, put bones into the water, you wonder where you can gather the strength to spoon the hot soup into his mouth, after he is washed and dried and wrapped in a blanket on a kitchen chair and asked to tell you what happened, what went wrong, who hit who first, knowing that later when he is sleepy he will ask you to tell a story.

How many years will you have to fake compassion, tell him it is all right to be human, to aim his goals a little lower, that not everyone will like him and that's okay. And you wash the dishes, resigned you will have to tell him another story tomorrow, this little boy who will never grow up, this little shit who says it hurts so much he must be bad; and you take his hand in yours and try not to crush it in your grip and lead him to a walk in the park until he forgets who he is and ceases to haunt you for awhile. Though when the stable blooms from your armpits and your clothes become too tight, when even the sunshine from the walk wears off, and one hand is hot and the other cold, and from where you sit you hear a clicking from the computer, while the incandescent light sputters, you know that he is back.

On a Theory of Causality

Nothing runs itself.
You can never sit back
and let habit or routine
substitute for intelligence or choice:
the universe is an accident.

The stars' dust falling over us,
always and forever,
is a result of countless accidents;
the fixed stars crawling overhead
through immeasurable spans of time
are an accident.

Overhead is an accident in the sky...
the warp of any wind...
the lemon tree in Crete
burdened with lemons,
so big and tart
you could bite through the skin into the flesh
tasting no bitterness...
a cat's fig-like brain
encased in its flexible skeleton—
all accidents.

I am an accident with the meter running,
pretending a destination
while idling in the car,
presuming a direction
because the pulse bumps along;
but the Shiva spirit is ruthless;
even now, her accidents are coming
or about to come out of the dark.

Somewhere on a tree-lined street
where life is lived simply,
its rhythms relaxed by a slower tempo,
its values sired by the Bible and propinquity,
where the spring's first blossoms
shroud the car and carpet the road,
I touch the starter button
wondering what will break.

Doppelganger

You are the stranger
seen at funerals or weddings,
whose clothes are too tight,
whose shoes are scuffed
and worn at the heel,
who eats too much at night,
who, if met at a party,
is accorded respect,
and at the poker game is grateful
for solicitude from others.

In windows glinting from the sun,
you see your face
as someone else might,
unadorned and perishable,
someone who does not recognize
he has become the person
in the bathroom mirror.

The man he sees is collected
from descriptions of other witnesses;
that picture in his wallet mislaid,
the boy in the baseball cap,
left in an automat
while looking for something;
so that years later,
(and this is you now)

that boy becomes a fiction,
a figment of the imagination,
a character in *Boys' Life*,
without compass and penknife
who is lost in the forest.

As the bald spot spreads
and the knees buckle,
you stop
to let the elder go ahead,
only to realize it is you
blinking at a world making haste,
unable to keep up,
looking over your shoulder
to catch a glimpse of the man
you have become.

You wonder about him,
regard him as a potential friend,
whose views you would know,
whose story you would learn,
who would take your measure
and find you satisfactory:
someone who would honor you,
someone you could love,
the one who would share
the center-cut of the day.

Lament

I mocked myself
in the caves
on the rocks by the shore
I held myself
in scorn and contempt
and wept
in the vineyards
for I was sore and tired
and the music left me
and I lay down without rest
and rose without hope
and went to a shallow place
to dwell among slaves
and ate the corn
that had turned to stone
and saw no reflection
when I peered into the well
and my clothes stank
from the seed I spent
upon the ground
and I crushed grapes
from the vineyard
to make the bitter wine
and drank it all my life
and they buried me
with stained feet
and a red mouth.

My Present Condition

There were periods, of course,
when I was sane,
for this, you will have to take my word.
But something occurred I could not face:
a sense of sin.
Pretty pink ribbons stitched to my hands
jerked them about;
my penis crawled off like a caterpillar
as I slept;
I smelled urine on the cake.

I craved order,
but the Empire fell
and the last senator was dragged
spitting from his chair
by a barbarian—
I cannot face the decision
to begin and begin and begin...
The moths assembling on the trees
look for a way to get in;
and my gentle cat, driven to distraction
by this, grows thin.

I cannot comfort him.

At Twenty-Five

On a day when I felt not so well,
I willingly went to the hospital.
My sister left me
where she stood behind the grate
and waved goodbye in a loose nightgown.
Policemen were there who came along;
so many, I did not count and was amazed.

They assigned a room
that was mostly bare—
somewhere to spend the night.
Because I wanted to leave my bed,
they tied me down, their faces red,
the straps around
my shoulders, hips and legs.

When a bloated nurse, looking strange,
fed me cold food, I grew afraid.
The mashed potatoes ran with blood,
the meat with fetid excrement,
while the asparagus had a sour taste.
Eating a spoonful, I left the plate
and begged to go to the john.
A urinal was brought instead;
I wet my legs, my knees, the bed.

So I passed the night,
writhing and dreaming,
and every so often, the nurses came
to give me a needle, to help me rest.
And so, I passed the night.
It was the day of my birth,
my twenty-fifth year—
I swear I remember,
amid the fear and tearing,
the dreams of dying,
the curse of healing;
I had never been here.

II

Common Knowledge

How many years have you hunted the Snark,
as if in used bookstores,
at the bottom of a dusty bin,
you would find your own book
and reclaim from oblivion
years of research and close reasoning.
Instead, you see what you puzzled out
disappear even from the footnotes
and pass into common knowledge—
one in a series of givens.

Hank wears his Micky Mouse costume
to the Halloween party;
he wants nothing else than to be liked.
But you want something more from the world
and the world is hard on you
and stingy.

If it is your life, it is convenient
to maintain an apartment
in one of the world's great cities,
stay in touch with fashion
if only to know how others perceive you,
tread warily among those whose comfort
depends on your indulgence.
Leave no felicity unacknowledged;

mention Lois Borden, the blind woman
you helped at the post office
fill out her Medicare forms
and made between two envelopes
the space she signed her name,
but don't let your mind stray
from your side of the story—
the hard fact that the other person lied,
or misrepresented an important detail.

Sneer at no one, not the dwarf
in the Rembrandt painting,
nor Sally, the Asian giantess
who rides the office elevator,
and take the advice from Bernice,
who works beside you in the vineyards,
and has been passed over, time after time:
"Don't wait for official recognition—
approve of yourself."

So when it comes your turn
to feed the convalescent
whose condition is terminal,
be sure to feed yourself an equal ration.
What looks like dust on the grapes
is a mold that sweetens them.

The Ice Age

Silent for so long,
his tongue became a glacier,
and a tree grew from his mouth,
its trunk in his throat,
its roots fastened to his heart.
It had its seasons and bouquet of blossoms
and canopy of leaves in the spring
and flock of birds and color in the fall,
and though the glacier's mantle reached his heart,
the tree did not die and he survived.
Instead, it grew gnarled
and tunneled by squirrels,
and woodpeckers drummed it,
and tree spiders slung webs
when the leaves were gone
and lightning singed it,
and storms tore its branches,
and in winter,
stars poked through its bare branches,
and winter light gave it a metallic sheen,
but the glacier could not kill it.
He survived because the tree grew from him
and how the tree survived was a miracle.

Fall

When my second teeth came in, I was fortunate,
though I had just two pair of trousers for school,
and the bathroom mirror showed a gap-toothed fellow
of indeterminate age,
and I brought the teeth home to put under my pillow,
hoping for a quarter the next day. I slept soundly,
no more had I put my head down, than it was morning,
trampling the yellow leaves, brown leaves, red leaves,
up to my thighs on our street that ran all the way
to the factories of Railroad Ave., coming home
for a dinner of beans and bread and the burgundy
leaves tumbling from the beech and sycamore
trees, watching the V shapes of birds that
cut across our sky in Paterson, going south.

Labor Day

Outside in September,
the lawns are being mowed
as if the summer would never end.
Machines munch ragweed and clover
and the mower's cough behind the house
seems to come from between the walls.
A mild dog haunts the street
waiting to be petted,
and the cuckold dragging out the trash
wears the antlers of his lodge.

But the newspaper thudding on the stair
reports a world beyond imagining—out there.
It counts the sirens in the night
accumulating by the hour,
wailing through the sprawling city.
Among our quiet happenings here,
there are few misgivings,
only the press of sensible things,
close and comfortable, within reach—
although the immigrant Asian
seen from the bus,
her arms thrown over her knees,
squatting on the corner, disagrees.

The dense light from a humid day
shimmers in the late afternoon
making shadows fall like rubber mats
across the floor,
and somewhere a clock-radio trips
a talk show at the wrong hour,
a tall tale
about the dark side of the moon;
as an astronaut, in formal dress,
walks silently
on the ceiling of the room.

Coats

Many coats clog the closet:
the old coats, the worn coats,
coats that got smaller, the torn coats,
the stained coats, the coats never worn,
or worn too often with no respect.

Gone now are the festive coats
we donned when young to be in fashion,
coats left on the bench at the bus station,
or in the railroad restroom.
Coats loaned like books
that were never returned;
coats given to charity,
now worn by the wino in the alley.

Out they go, all of them:
coats that kept us warm,
that we grew into;
coats with a nostalgia about them:
coats from the Service days,
from the horse-racing days,
on sale in flea markets,
hanging on racks,
folded and laid away,
disposed of in stacks,
jettisoned with the bilge

to drift in our memories,
in the currents of time and tide,
when the choice to be different was once ours
and is ours no more.

The Music of the Spheres

Those who can hear know
that to follow it is impossible.
The note is lost too soon
amid the boiler-room racket
that billions make.
But that melody, caught
almost out of hearing,
sings us to birth and death.
It doesn't matter
how long you must wait
or how seldom the strains
carry close enough to catch,
you may yet hear its pennant snap
on a breezy day, or feel its warmth
on your back, reminding us
we cannot be reduced to a definition,
that some aroma wafts past us,
some freedom lifts over us and away.
It will come too far and in-between
to be called now and then,
but for all that, there,
among the everything else
we must endure and forgive.

The Lion's Mouth

Any resident lion will do—
you push past the shrieking children,
the attendant placing fresh meat,
the plump woman who smokes
beside the child with crooked features,
the digressions of bystanders,
still talking of the leopard;
for there is always a leopard,
a cheetah, a lynx, a tiger,
and the water buffaloes, so beautiful,
still as marble in their habitat.
Lions themselves are a cliquey pride,
bent on homogeneity.
Eventually putting off togetherness,
they go their own way:
each becomes a hermit on the hunt,
until there is only one lion,
the one in front of you,
the one you walk miles not to meet,
spend years in hiding to avoid,
yet expect at every turn,
dream about monotonously,
go about dreading, there at last,
and you offer your head,
the only offering there is,
putting it in his mouth

waiting for him to swallow,
submissive and beyond hope,
reaching for a last moment,
however brief,
when you possess yourself once more.

The Gatekeeper

Because he didn't understand
and couldn't think his sister dead,
he hid behind an open door.
For years his mother would prove
she was right.
There would be sacred days
when they would visit the grave.
He'd wear his father's helpless look
and share the blame,
and sit behind a girl in school
with the same name.

Because he didn't understand,
he became tangled in alternatives
that bore no significance
and wore down his resistance,
often listening to his own breathing
and pinching his arms until they were numb:
he liked flowered wallpaper,
tiny dolls with porcelain legs,
anything in a corner to blunt its shape.

Though he did understand
the responsibility had to be met.
Always thinking of that bare room
vacant of life

even as a grown man
discussed it with his wife:
Death denies any certification
and because it does not dwindle,
waits in a cold draft
between a doorway and open window.

Because there was much to understand,
he had semesters of thought
where life's botany was redefined
and a book of phone numbers underlined
after his wife died; he wrote a will,
drew a pension, bought a dog,
would forget to pay the bills.
He came to know it wasn't his fault
by growing old,
as he ceased to remember who he was.

Disillusion at 2AM

So there you are, past fifty,
warehoused in a tenement anthill
with a tick-tick heart condition
ready to risk another examination,
but your feet don't fit their shoes
and the lower back always hurts;
do you really want to know?

What you assume has a half-life
decays, fuses, fits an atomic scale.
Last summer's promise
vanishes in the farmer's almanac,
transforms into a chronic insomnia
when you peer at the sickle moon
stranded in sub-lunar night.

Then put ice cubes in a glass
and pour an ounce of scotch
from the plastic cup
that measures the cough medicine,
and raise a toast
to the overheating planet,
its squalls of cleansing rain
and spells of lucid weather.

Now, as you consider the recent dead,
roll the glass along your head to
cool the rising fever there,
and wonder in what other rooms
there are those, like you, who are awake,
their eyes bleary with double vision,
their hearts clouded with fickle weather
their lives a frozen lake.

So toss the night waiting for sleep
as needles of light search the heavens,
the floodlights' numb fingers
probing the coastline of your dreams,
the foghorn's phlegm in the throat,
the tide rising,
the wreckage floating in.

III

The Chicken Coops of Lewis Street

For Neil Monda (died July 21, 1953)

You said little toward the end
beside the radiator in your rocking chair,
deep into your atheism.
The doctor visited every two weeks,
put leeches on your arm,
spoke Italian,
and passed the time of day;
you cheated on your diet
as soon as he went away.

The family tells stories of your strength.
How you carried a stove on your back
to a newlywed's house
with the fire still in it,
or when you worked on the docks in Naples
and carried a pair of hundred-fifty-pound sacks of grain
while everyone else was content to carry one.
In my memory you still fill a doorway.

Mother handed you her paycheck
until the week before she married
at the age of thirty-three;
you gave her an allowance.
As a girl she hid in the shed
for days, staying out of your way,
when she cut my uncle's hand,

and she remembers Aunt Julia
kneeling on olive pits to do her homework
when she came home with a bad report card.

You didn't allow English at the dinner table,
though you read *Les Miserables* to Grandmother
over and over, while she cried at the sad parts,
refusing the Fascists
who wanted her golden ring for Mussolini,
tending her rosebush when she passed away.

You taught me to eat raw garlic,
the core of the apple,
the peels of oranges and lemons.
When I'd jump and caper
impatient to grow up
you'd call me to your rocking chair
and holding me by the ear
make the crazy circle with your finger
and tell me in broken English:
"Nobody home!"

The night you died I dreamed
your heavy footsteps
creaked up the stairs of our old house
and slowly came into my room,
and standing over my bed

with a stern look on your face
you threw darts into my chest.
When I awoke the next morning,
your bed was empty.

Your chicken coops are gone;
I tore them down one summer
when the neighbor next door complained
to the Board of Health—
he wouldn't have dared when you were alive.
Nothing is left now but the cement floor
and most of that is breaking up.
The grapevine died a few years ago
and the garden went to weeds;
only the peppermint survived
overwhelming the path to the garbage shed.

Nothing's left of your old order.
St. Rocco's club has been taken over
by a new wave of immigrants.
No living relatives remain in Italy,
only the photograph in the cellar
of you and your brother,
my other Grandfather,
you fought with
and wouldn't speak to for fifteen years.

Last Year's Overcoat

As a truck unloads the greenhouse flowers
from the old priests' home,
as a mild winter uncrates the sun,
as I turn the corner at the flower shop
without a job
and start out,
a folded newspaper,
a roll of Lifesavers,
a road map in the glove compartment,
I encounter,
after the first stop light,
the moron traffic going nowhere,
the cars double-parked,
the cars waiting to turn at intersections,
the school bus.

At the office,
I do the expected things,
filling out forms,
next of kin, three friends,
not related,
who will testify under the third degree
I'm an all right guy.
An interview no toilet training prepared me for,
the interviewer on an egg hunt:
my nervous breakdowns,

the worker's compensation for hernia,
the jobs I was fired from.
The evidence is too great.
I am unfit,
a cosmic mistake.
Like a split pen nib
I make an illogical stutter.
Grateful for dismissal,
I leave with a flutter
and settle for lunch in a small diner.

I loiter on the corner.
The deadly sin of sloth
has made me an organ grinder's monkey.
I go into a bookstore
and spend the day
mixing the neat arrangement of books.
Buying nothing,
I leave under suspicion.

Not wanting to go home,
I merge into the homebound traffic,
going nowhere,
driving around the library,
driving along the river,
driving into the cemetery.

The Cognoscenti Lament the Dollar's Decline

All that happens, happens here:
the FM radio plays "The Planets" by Holst
and lunch is laid on the table...
The same newspapers, the familiar brand names
broadcast at the commercial breaks
and the news pronounces its usual woe:
the cognoscenti lament the dollar's decline.

Foucault's pendulum swings due to physical law,
available throughout the cosmos,
a child's tantrums test his parents' patience,
and our parents die when we least expect it
while much besides can be anticipated:
the peanut left in the ashtray will be rancid.

Awhile back, a glacier cracked in Antarctica
launching an iceberg the size of Rhode Island
into the South Pacific where it raised eyebrows,
but the thing sizzled to a chip.

Perhaps, in another galaxy
a Black Hole exists
waiting to devour our solar system
and reel back our yesterdays and tomorrows
in a quick-time clip.

But for now, the cat is vomiting again,
the women through the wall
are doing their thing with the whip
and next door,
Mr. Kelly is carried away in a body bag,
dead from cancer—
I never got the courage to knock.
A hall light burns out near the elevator
and Rebecca scolds the Super,
who chews the straw he has taken up
since he quit smoking.

To Someone I Cannot See Anymore

Your backyard
has gone to weeds.
Your man is gone.
The letter from your daughter
is old, old news.
Now you only approximate yourself.

You're always reading
half a dozen books.
The bowl of wax grapes
gathers dust on the table,
and the wash on the line
rain or shine
hangs a week.

I'll bring my friend
to the sour plant
with purple leaves
upon the window,
though you'll not let us in.
You're nothing special,
still, I feel
the responsibility to try.

I know a man
retired on a pension
who looks at his garden all day
and sees you pass
your half-open kitchen door
but hasn't a thing to say
about you.
I'll visit him.

Troubled Sleep

You lie in a field where grass bends in the wind
and parasols of dandelions are knocked askew.
Pollen hangs a musk in the air,
while fireflies are tongues of flame in the dusk.
Though you want to hold what remains of the day,
cries are heard that have no source;
the moon bleeds like the rind of a pomegranate.
A faceless child wriggles through your dreams,
and you wake in a sweat,
unable to remember if you are here
or somewhere else...
The map on the wall shows everything
that is known or has been explored;
there is no rent in the whole design where
wonder can shine through an open window,
and you watch the digital clock,
a Geiger counter pulsing in the dark.

Storm Warning

A pause in the music
and the news report
apprises us of the hurricane
moving swiftly up the coast.
Over toast and coffee,
we hear essential facts relate
the death and havoc in its wake
as authorities facilitate
the evacuation of survivors.

September shines in our lives
like a medallion from a lost culture,
bestowing its redemption
through a new Pentecost,
but our escape
cannot be foretold by any revelation.

And now, after a break,
the music resumes,
and we must consider
our raincoats and rubbers,
the possible flood in the cellar,
a slate gray sky
and the sight of many birds
fleeing northward.

Monday

There are times when I want to walk
into another life: find new pursuits,
a fresh set of obligations, different friends,
another's wife. When there's nowhere to go
I haven't hurried to a zillion times,
when the story I tell myself is stale,
and even pride is dull,
when attention fixates on bodily decline;
the walk to cure the back
and return feeling to my numb foot
occurs while someone else appears
along the way to Snug Harbor, at first indistinct,
but coming closer on the shore road,
and I would become him, the instant he passes,
going toward the direction I came.
It'd be a second chance, another beginning,
my mind a grid of new affiliations,
opinions, memories, hopes, and fears.
I'd be moving into another's arms.
What would she be like? Aching to see her,
I press forward; there's excitement in my walk.
Someone stops to ask the time.
Where is *he* going? But I become afraid,
for how will I know when I get there,
there may be no one waiting, no terminus.
The way forward appears a trackless waste...

If I had the faith, all would be well,
but there's no way of knowing,
only some benches, here and there, to rest.
It becomes clear, should I find the door
to this new life, the stair to climb,
the key to open that door,
and if a surprise party were waiting for me,
it would be much like the life I left:
a rush of excitement, then a coming to terms,
an arousal in the dawn, then an evening shower
to revive the spirit, something not done,
done badly or put off, the obligation denied,
the compliment unacknowledged.
And I am walking in two directions
that lead to the same place,
as the day ahead stretches—the morning long,
the night coming an eternity,
where the new bed will be waiting,
a harbor of safety for small boats
bobbing on rough seas.

No Balloons

Morning, and the usual worries begin—
the heart fluttering and skipping beats,
the terrible joy, the intensity of happiness
at being singled out and spoken to,
the moment of connection with another.
It has always been that way:
a burden never acknowledged;
only now I assume responsibility...
Today, I will be fifty-seven
with no balloons at the office,
though I am respected and liked,
and that's something.
Even Bea, quiet to a fault, gets balloons;
everybody has somebody
to give them balloons for their birthday.
I should scrawl on the bulletin board,
"Today is my birthday, get me some balloons."
The world was circled by a balloon today,
crossing 9 degrees longitude
as the Spring Equinox arrives with its equipoise,
and the gangway lifts from the ramp,
the ferry sliding into the anonymous waters
of the Verazzano Strait,
the passengers braced for the journey,
their morning tiredness throwing long shadows
down the rows of benches.

The Burning Bed

You smuggle yourself in here
and find me vague and distracted.
You do not belong in this place,
and I cannot fathom why they let you in.
You say you have come to spend the night,
though I do not let you sleep,
for people are setting the bed on fire.
Each time I begin to doze,
they gather to set it ablaze.
You say I am a peaceful man,
but we both need sleep.
How weary your voice sounds:
"Sleep knits the raveled sleeve, Bob."
Not wanting to be more trouble,
I bid you goodnight and turn away
with the bed engulfed in flames.

Pushing Sixty

Catching every virus in winter's revolving door
and surviving to hoist my corporeal frame
two flights up the subway, arthritic limbs creaking;
then passing the flowers I thought to buy
my wife when I remembered she is allergic
to several varieties, though which I forget.
I find the unhealthy hot-dog, clutching
its paper wrapping and squirting mustard,
for my trip home among the commuters,
salutary to my taste and easy on my wallet,
subsisting, as I am, on a pension, the engine's
groan pulsing the ferry toward the waiting bus
I will catch to the summit of Hamilton Ave.,
and if that isn't enough (my weariness screams it is),
I must query my email, finger my word processor
and study for several graduate courses at once—
comparing my life to a hermit's is no longer an option—
but now the crisis I must weather is can I last
this semester, or shall I bolt for parts unknown
and appear in dark glasses at some foreign airport
and hail a cab to a remote monastery and hide there
among the missing until the coast is clear.

IV

Dream of My Father

The morning of your death
I had a dream:
I leave home in driving rain
following your second wife
to her widow's house,
go through your clothes for small change,
do not find what I'm owed
but leave, my pockets bulging.
You stand in the doorway
holding Easter palm and wearing a *ramos*,
and tell me to split the change with my sister.
In the elevator I see the neighbor's boy
and give him the handful of coins,
but do not utter a word of encouragement.
Like you, I am a miser.

A Few Photographs

Head inclined, my father
seems to be listening, but isn't.
He hands me a photograph,
wrinkled and faded,
from his wallet:

"These are pictures of my son...
he was a Marine...."

He lets me hold a snapshot
taken thirty years ago
when he was my age.

"My brother died in the war...
he won two Silver Stars...."

"I remember, Dad,
  seeing Uncle Neil in uniform..."

My father is not listening.
He's adrift on an ice floe
with the photographs
being drawn out to sea.
He looks them over,
not missing the one I hold.
Later, he puts them back
to take out when we next meet.

They are what he has kept—
they flash and flare
in the numbing cold,
matches struck in polar regions,
where the hands lose all feeling
until the fingers stiffen
over what was left to kindle.

Now the world sticks to his skull
like napalm
and absently
he stares at TV
where a bombed-out road
in some endless war
stretches to infinity.

Old Men in the Park

The old men sit in the park
over checkers and chess;
they are always the same.
On days grown dark
against fretful skies,
we can see them glowing faintly
with a cold luster,
far from the yaw of junks
where famine sculpts a myriad of faces,
and far from the interrogation rooms
where victims call their torturer, "Doctor."

The old men swap stories under the trees;
their malice lodges with roaches
in stale cupboards, nesting
in raw wounds with maggots.

We hear those stories from the cradle,
renew them in the flowering of our sex,
sprout their pulpy fruit in our dreams—

I know them by heart.

Salutations

Stranger, we are unhooked
from what moored us;
we are not now as we were
in that Annus Mirabilis,
when the taste of the apple
filled our mouths with its sweetness.
Naked, Shelley stalked the house
to invite his muse to sing,
but we haven't his great heart,
and we live the buried life,
chewing the sour cud of respectability.
The thin fluid pumped in our bodies
holds us erect on fetid platforms,
pools in our feet as we wait for the late train,
identifies us as mammals.
I recognize your slouch, much like mine
among the waiting crowd. See my finger
raised in salute across the platform—
answer with yours.

Wire Mommy

Just when I have found the open door
to the burnt offering,
the steel talisman that thwarts the evil omen
and transfigures blighted youth
into middle-aged survivor,

Just when streaking tracers mark fields of fire
that interleave and intertwine, blend and merge,
engage and destroy,

Just when every partition of space echoes
with the mouth sewn shut,
when all things are possible to the pen
whose dried ink swirls with ridges,
there comes this earth dug for new graves,
moist clay and wet grass
shoveled over a coffin;

There comes this relief, my enemy,
now that you are dead,
and the world, emptied of your presence,
must find other horrors to inflict upon its children,
and your iron hand I hold, until mine withers,
begins its eternity of rust—that smile
of my final farewell.
You were always the stronger one,
my strength is what took hold and won't let go.

V

Traveling Through Wyoming

Nature is close here:
in the feathered tracks a small beast makes
over muddy ground,
in the talus silting a valley floor,
recording a mountain's long talk with God.

Here the eagle paints the world he circles
with his bloody eye,
diving once, then making off
with something still alive,
and the Black Oak kills the offspring
that try to sprout at its side.

From here, I send postcards to Brooklyn
where the blare of radios is always heard
from cruising cars,
and we wear each other's socks
swapped at the laundromat—
one size fits all,
while the fire hydrants pump water,
night and day,
as the hot summer beckons,
murderous and incendiary,
and the calm that would nourish,
cannot survive the wild diversity,
but must be dispensed

by prescription at drugstores
or obtained in jittery transactions
on street corners.

Wyoming slips behind
in the rear–view mirror—
a shrunken sky ahead
mounts above the reek of gasoline.

In the Heartland

for George Woodington

Released from the navy
when he learned to wet the bed,
he served his sentence of underdog,
combing the factory outlets for sales,
stalled on congested roads,
getting to the shore, now and then,
where he watched the swaying boats
moored in the cove.
Arc welding through the night,
he drove rivets that fit
a place of escape,
wiping the sweat from his receding hair,
punching out to sit with a beer,
then returning to a cluttered flat
to bag a lunch for the following day.
The law he obeyed, he paid and paid,
dreamed of winning the lottery
and went to sleep.

Still, a ragged fire licked his ears
with its flickering tongue.
A beast lunged within him
crashing the bounds of its kennel.
Stammering like Moses,
he dreamed of pressing his hands into stone,

but found the world ignored him
and contrived to leave it alone.
He disappeared into the heartland,
hid from sight, burrowed deep
and got lost there.
For days to come, we left the key in the box,
checked the papers, called the police,
wrapped up his affairs
and hoped he'd come back.

But what will life be like for him
should he emerge in the future?
Certainly, his personality will remain,
his features clear
after a moment of recognition
recalls them to us,
though can we explain
the journey he endured
wandering for years in the wilderness?

And yes, tell us if you can,
why he left so long ago
to tread the earth in foreign parts
leaving us all behind?

Cape Charles Library

An old church has been converted
to house a few shelves of books.
A cabinet displays trophies near the door,
and a stained-glass window is domed behind
the librarian.
It is said God never leaves
a house he once occupied;
the librarian knows this,
that is why there are flowers in the vase beside
her;
it is why children run around the stacks
looking like they leaped from a Winslow
Homer painting,
why the television broadcasting soap opera
is turned off when someone begins to write,
leaving the screen to reflect upon itself
like a praying nun,
and why the sun burns off the haze at last
over the Chesapeake Bay showing
all it has been hiding.

Hearing Mississippi Fred McDowell

He says only what he has to,
singing like no one else can,
peeling us like a hand of bananas,
the delta man with the fruit blossom smile
long accustomed to living in public
behind dark glasses.
Leaning back and pressing his lips hard
like he was by himself
letting it all come out
"you ought'a hear my white dog bark."
He shares nothing that is not ours,
first come first served,
a one-course meal of cement bricks
and pick your teeth with a claw hammer
and howl.

Freedom, New Hampshire

Matching a list against the computer,
the record scrolls to Freedom, New Hampshire.
Now what do they do in Freedom, New Hampshire?
Is there a general store with a video outlet?
A few streets, a handful of houses?
Does the graveyard show names from two centuries?
When it rains in Freedom,
does the old man rocking on the porch
still roll up his American flag?
On the outskirts of Freedom
(a small town like many others)
is there an inventor
with a shed full of contraptions?
Does a back hoe break the ground
on "sixty acres, more or less,"
where beavers build dams
and poison ivy is cleared with brush fire?
And is there a mountain south of Freedom
where a squatter huddled in his shack
looks steadily into the Milky Way?
Freedom is cut by a fold in the map
but you will find it;
follow the directions
straight to the end of the road.

Year of the Comet

for Luke

A heap of rags smelled of cleaning fluid;
the sun shone over the open sill
and the aroma of lilac wafted in;
butter cookies cooled on the counter.
His mother's hand steadied
his rubbery first steps
as the world began in earnest;
specks of iridescence filled the air.

Rug found a bone in the garden
and munched, a satisfied growl, below the window.
Burial sites have been discovered
that show men interred with their dogs
dating back 50,000 years;
that's 581 visits of Hailey's comet,
while Ursa Major spins like a flywheel
above the hemispheres.

VI

Sub Rosa

If there were no you,
to whom would I tell my dreams,
who would hear my longings?
I would swell up like a balloon
with all these things inside;
like a balloon the sidewalk mime
fashions into a dinosaur for a child,
eventually I would pop.
You, who keep me
as secure as the string on a balloon
that would drift off
and be swallowed by the sky,
you are only half aware of this.
And what do I do for you:
wash a few dishes,
empty the garbage,
shop for groceries?
My life is so easy
that I tremble
someday you will discover
my secret.

The Cat's Diet

"The cat," you say, "is getting thin..."
turned toward the scratching beast.
Oh, gentle lady, if he were thin,
you must leave the bowl
half-full for him.
Is it your double you seek
nostalgically trim?
Is it what you dream
while peering into the mist?
The flesh that resists
cannot be lost
by a magician's trick.
But I bite my lip
and still my tongue.
We all see omens
arching common sense
and patch as we can
a future full of hope
and try to summon
something useful to say
if we are asked one day.

A Spare Rib

We didn't need it after all,
though every man has his doubts.
Before Adam was cast into sleep,
the omission was discovered,
and God moved to amend His creation.

So it came to pass,
the dynasties of Asoka and Ptolemy
issued from the daughters of Seth and Sham
as did all seers and madmen.
Tonight the girls take you out
for a dinner of spare ribs—
eat hearty and make them glad.
You are thirty-five years old
and there is nothing spare about you.

Mr. Yeats' Song

As all men are frail,
a sack of fluid and fevers,
repelling the world step by step,
as each of them stops at times,
at times starts again in other directions,
who among them, even the flintiest,
is not guided by a woman
who sailed with Columbus
to places a flat-earther could never imagine,
who among them, even the unlucky
is not mended like a tablecloth
by her pliant hands,
is not cherished by her
and given reasonable work,
is not broken of bad habits
and hot tempers, is not honored,
does not owe a final blessing
when on his last legs?

The Sailor's Song

Before the equator in me subsides
into a lesser circle,
I hope to touch
the ocean salt of your blood.
Before the light of our red sun
dies in the eyes of a distant star,
I hope to come uneventful to your side—
a drunken sailor,
my boat splintered upon the rocks,
come to town to celebrate my life
and smart enough to point at the sky,
but unable to get enough
bent between your thighs.
And so full of pride
I offer half my life,
only to leave again with the tide,
to wake up dead
on the decks of the prairie
still dreaming, the sea
beneath the bow.
Before time turns the bone to ash,
I hoard this light,
light that floods your face,
light that pools your footsteps.
Before the day I was about to be,
you found your way,

behind my back
in some other order,
without me—
a great arc that springs ahead
into the searchlights darting.

Genesis

When you come to me,
Eve, all naked in innocence,
I reach to embrace you
as the sun presses my face,
birds call into my ears,
and water curls against my feet.
Somewhere in the garden
is a tree and a serpent;
but not here, not yet.
This is the crystal time
before watches and weather
when each animal
stumbles toward us
waiting to be named.

The Net

When you return from seeing your father
hooked to their machinery
like a fish tangled in the lines,
you are very tired,
tired of how life binds,
how its tasks consume.
But your life is a net
that you spread out
at the pier's end,
and mend thread by thread,
a net that catches the gathering sea
and lets most pass
in order to trap what sustains you.
It must be pulled up slowly
from the bottom.
The shoulders ache lifting it.
After it is emptied, spread to dry,
mollusks like teeth are pried loose
and seaweed is pulled off.
Then it rests waiting between immersions;
it waits spitting snails into the sand;
it sucks its teeth and waits in silence.

While You Wait

I reach my hand toward you;
see the lines branch on the palm,
a tree consumed as it reaches you.
A child is somewhere in its branches;
he has my father's name,
and his face is red from crying—
Listen to him howl.
It is everyone's cry of pain
in the keening of the wind
as it blows
through the pale palms of the leaves.
Its psalms are sung every night
somewhere under the conceiving moon.

Reaching Out

My friend, we walk arm in arm
back to our apartment,
leaving the doughnut shop's
warm patch of sunlight upon the table.
You do not seem to mind
I have run out of steam
stretching to keep up with you,
you who reach out to those around you,
resilient and poised while age approaches,
relentless and irrevocable,
as vibrant as you were at twenty.

VII

Whiskey Priest

His breath a blast
of onions and tequila,
when he brought the bath water
to our family on Saturdays,
being the last to bathe.
He kept the ends of candles in his pockets,
a rosary rolled in his pants leg,
when they came to get him,
still tipsy from having finished
the holy wine.
Nowadays, the local padre
comes by Jeep
to our far-off mountain;
he is lean and sober,
and tells us of Christ and Marx,
but I would exchange his earnestness
for the old rogue anytime,
who carried fish line to catch lizards,
and who loved the bed of Isadora,
and whose feet,
the tortured feet they left him,
shone like the bronze feet of St. Paul
in the Basilica of San Isidro.

New Stone Egg

I came into your cell
and found the jacket you forgot,
distinct and foreign to my eyes.
You were gone;
the plumb-line measured
where you cut through the floor.
What effort it must have taken
with the thin gruel we fed you.
I looked at the walls
where you tallied time
in decades not in years.
You dropped no hints of your plan,
except the note, after your flight,
left under the stone egg
you used as a paperweight,
written with humor, a flair for words,
a bold signature.
But why was it addressed to me?
I never liked you, didn't care
about the wife and kids you never saw,
took every advantage over you I could.
I still hope to discover
something I wasn't prepared for,
something that will land you back inside.
What remains is my shadow
burnt into your mirror

from where I watched you
all those years. Thank you.
You left a clean cell
for the next prisoner;
it will be an inspiration.
His sentence is a long one,
but you taught him patience,
the patience to sit each day
looking toward where I sat.

The Clay Foot

If we found a stone elephant
with only three feet
where a dark tide threw it
when the culture died that made it,
a clay foot could be added
to make it stand again.
Then we might see it
as those it had shouldered
to view the sacred dead,
sweating stone droplets with elephant strength,
pushing a petrified tree with its head.

But only the foot survives
from which we infer the whole
lost so long ago,
round and white with tons of weight
supported by its toes,
and we still hear the roar as it fell
and the ring of the shot that brought it down
as the reek of gunpowder persists,
rising over steep cliffs in our granite sleep.

Courting the Muse, Two Visits

I

Her puffy white foot, pulled from its sock,
props on the chair. It flexes and curls,
inclined toward the fire on this winter day,
where a splinter lifts, sparks and goes out,
an illusion swallowed by the dark.

Her favors issue to you
from the roots exposed by a fallen tree,
from the colander of rinsed vegetables,
touching you like her hand drawn from a mitten
and held to you in honesty and trust.

It is never what you can imagine
but always unexpected, random,
the chance prod
in a universe of gears and pulleys
that bolsters your resolve,
granting the grace for a deep breath
you have been holding forever.

You see her skipping rope in the schoolyard,
or among the aromas of the spice shop,
her socks rolled down,
standing over a barrel of lentils,
the beads cupped in her small hands:
you think of her the whole day.

II

No amount of fasting or good works
can lure her; suddenly she is there;
grateful and eager,
you offer your best chair
and today she takes it
though usually she stands.

She taunts you for your inconstant heart,
saying faith in the weather report
lost more battles than rough terrain,
laughing at you as you close the door
when she leaves to make her rounds.

She needs nothing from you
not even your reverence.
She contends whatever you write
runs with the sap of sentiment,
aims to please, indulges itself,
smells of sawed wood in a workshop.

She says you are one of those
who carry sets of keys,
many whose purpose has been forgotten,
one burdened with the weight of time,
with doors long since rusted shut,
or demolished by the wrecking ball,

doors that swing wide revealing
the party within still going on,
where your name has just been called
and people you have erased wait for you.

You watch her disappear
behind an office building,
your small pieties unnoticed,
unacknowledged, always knowing
you are two old friends
who have betrayed each other
after they betrayed themselves.

Franklin's Kite

Will someone offer us a light?
We have been searching everywhere;
werewolves are howling in the night.

Pascal's wager is now thought trite;
see Hume for reasons, should one care.
Has anyone ever seen the light?

Kepler put heaven out of sight;
quarks are hardly even there.
Werewolves are lurking in the night.

The storm has swallowed Franklin's kite;
the milling crowd has a vacant stare.
Will someone lead us to the light?

Freud wants to curb our appetites;
Heisenberg leaves us in despair.
Werewolves are circling in the night.

Skinner's box and Kierkegaard's fright
shadow the mocking face of Voltaire.
Will Buber lead us to the light?
Werewolves have found us in the night.

Chinese Novel

Open on the seat, a Chinese novel
left on the subway at Canal Street—
a pavilion brushed on its cover,
a line of mountains feathered in,
a teardrop moon, a handful of stars.
The pages are a true wonder,
rows of pictographs
arouse a desire to understand,
to pause over each character
and discern its differences.
The spine is flattened,
the pages all turned,
whatever saga fills it
left for someone else.
Perhaps, in another life,
this karma dispensed,
I will enter, a hero and polyglot,
scan the places to laugh,
to shake my head,
study intently its final pages,
absorbing the author's impressions,
each glyph dissolving like a lozenge,
each flavor—salt or sweet or sour—
washing over me until the last image
reveals its enigmatic meaning.

Member of the Family

My sister's new dog pees
on my trouser leg. How cute!
He is marking his territory
and I am his domain.
A Nazi dog that would rule,
needing *lebensraum*,
he wears the black sweater
of the Hitler Youth.
But I am exaggerating.
The pee will wash off,
as will the dog smell.
Who knows but the dog
will want to lick off my smell.
They tell me his name.
It is a one syllable word,
but I cannot remember.
I sit patiently, until I can leave.
Everyone is looking at the dog
as he chews a puppy toy
in the middle of the room.
I can't wait to revisit my sister,
and Fred—his name is Fred!—
will jump on me again,
his nose against my testicles.
Oh, let that day be soon.

Thank You

I want to thank my wife, Robin, for being my editor for these last fifty years. Thank you, too, to Michael Carman, for her invaluable generosity and skills as the final editor and proofreader of this book. Finally, thank you to my poetry group—Robin Locke Monda, Michael Carman, Victoria Hallerman and Lisa Rhoades—for their ongoing support and insight as I worked to bring these poems to the page.

About the Type

This book was set in Minion Pro, an Adobe Originals digital typeface designed by Robert Slimbach for Adobe Systems in 1990. Slimbach's design was inspired by late-Renaissance typefaces, which are noted for their elegance, beauty and readablity. Minion was created primarily for text use. According to Adobe, "Minion combines the aesthetic and functional qualities that make text type highly readable with the versatility of digital technology."

Made in the USA
Middletown, DE
02 April 2021